Book of Wisdom

For more information about this and other books
and services, please contact us at:

centerforinnerawakening@gmail.com

www.centerforinnerawakening.com

416-737-9699

Book of Wisdom

A Simple Book for Spiritual Growth

Mohmood Valimohamed

Moonlight Books

Book of Wisdom - A Simple Book for Spiritual Growth

First Print   2001
Second Print   2003

National Library of Canada Cataloguing in Publication

Valimohamed, Mohmood
        Book of Wisdom : a simple book for spiritual growth
/ Mohmood Valimohamed.

ISBN   1-894806-10-7

        1.Spiritual life. 2. Self-actualization (Psychology)—
Religious aspects. I. Title.

BL624.V35 2003   291.4   C2003-902609-4

Quantity discounts available on our website
www.centerfordivinity.com

The Author and Publisher can be reached at
info@centerfordivinity.com

Contents

Dedication

This book is dedicated to all the individuals who are interested in spiritual growth. At some point during our lifetime our soul prompts us to ask "What is my purpose on Earth?" We start looking for answers as our curiosity grows. May the journey of your soul be guided by eternal light.

Acknowledgements

First and foremost I would like to acknowledge my gratitude to my mother Nurnihar. She gave me the inspiration to write this book. She has always been a great source of wisdom for me and my family.

I would like to thank my best friend Nuruddin for his tremendous support. He has played a key role in the production of this book. He has also supported me during critical moments in my life. May the light of God always guide him.

A special thanks goes to my sister-in-law Shalina and my brother Karim. Shalina has supported not only myself but also my entire family. During critical moments in our life, she has repeatedly given us tremendous support. Her kind heart is a great blessing to us. Karim has also assisted in the design of this book. Thank you for everything.

I would like to take this opportunity to thank Ami of "For Home Based Office" for her great efforts. She is truly a genuine person and has worked very hard in the making of this and other books.

I would like to thank my younger brother Altaf for his contribution toward this book. He has provided support in various areas in the production of this book.

Suffering: A Blessing in Disguise

There is no individual on earth who has not suffered at one point or another. Suffering takes place in a variety of ways. Health problems can have a serious impact on your day-to-day life. Limited resources cause strain. Complications resulting from family situations can seriously affect your soul.

From the time we are in our mother's womb, we are fighting to survive. The nine months spent in the womb are not a very comfortable time for the soul. We are upside down in a very small area, with hardly any room to move, and subject to many heat waves.

Before conception, the soul who is about to be born through the chosen mother comes to the mother to ask for permission. The mother is subconsciously aware of the spirit coming into her womb. There is a very strong connection between the baby and the mother. During the first few months of pregnancy, the infant's spirit visits the mother's womb several times. This is a very special stage in a mother's life. She starts picking up messages from the child's soul in the form of dreams, promptings, and visions. The ability to pick up these messages may vary from one mother to another. The greater the mother's ability to perceive the subtle messages, the clearer will be the communication with her infant's spirit.

The infant's spirit comes out of the spirit world and enters the world of matter through the mother. There is extraordinary freedom in the spirit world. You are fully aware of your past and your future. You are able to travel from one universe to another.

When the soul enters the womb, it loses all the freedom that was in the spirit world. Because of this sudden transfer into the material world, the unborn child starts to kick and complain. The mother has the unique ability to feel the pain of her child.

After a few months of gestation, the soul remains in the mother's womb. This is a very special time for the mother. There are two souls in one body. An aura glows in the mother's face. Mothers should take advantage of this special time and meditate as much as possible. The potential for spirituality dramatically increases since there are two spiritual lights in the body.

The infant starts to adapt. A curtain is placed in the memory of the soul so that when it is ready to come into this world, it will not remember any past actions.

Suffering is a blessing in disguise. Through suffering your soul comes closer to God. Suffering is the way to enlightenment. There are many special types of suffering available. You can experience suffering as a father, mother, sister, brother, grandparent, and dear friend.

It is said that when a mother gives birth to her child, the mother's labour cries are heard through the seven heavens. Motherhood is a stage in evolution that begins at the moment a woman becomes pregnant. After her child is born, the mother's compassion and love for her infant dramatically increase. She is now ready to sacrifice her health, wealth, security —everything- for the sake of her child.

Motherhood enriches the soul in a variety of ways. A mother is a symbol of mercy, compassion and grace. A mother displays tolerance, patience, love, and warmth. Imagine all these qualities united in one individual. Before the ancient sages came to earth, they were granted permission by their mothers. If there were no mothers, there would be no spiritual guidance. There would be no structure in society. Mothers help all great souls reach enlightenment. Without a mother, enlightenment would not be possible.

When we become physically ill, we rush to the doctor. Often the doctor tells us that we have a virus, which does not respond to medication. The doctor's advice is to let our body fight the virus and heal itself. The more we let the body fight, the stronger our immune system will be and the healthier we will become. In order to grow stronger, we must suffer and fight the infection first.

In a similar manner, in order for the soul to grow, it must suffer first. It has to be given a chance to suffer in as many ways as possible. The greater the suffering, the richer the soul becomes. During periods of suffering, you explore the depths of your soul. The divine is hidden inside the heart. There are many layers of suffering that we must penetrate in order to develop spiritually. After you have fought a virus, you will feel healthier than ever before. You earned your sense of well-being. Similarly once you have endured suffering, you are richer, wiser, and more spiritual. In the end you will say that it was worth it; you are now one step closer to God.

A father goes through a similar type of suffering. He is constantly under pressure to provide for his family. He may feel that the mother of his children has sacrificed a great deal for her infants. Once a father's eyes rest on his newborn child, a transformation takes place in his soul. He realizes that a brand new life has entered his own. It's a miracle to hold such a tiny being in his hands. The ego dissolves. From that point onwards, he says to himself, "I have to be the one to provide for this little one. This is a great responsibility."

You don't always suffer because of your past karmas. Suffering can come because of many other factors. You may have chosen an illness before your birth so that the world may benefit from your illness. Your illness can act as a safety valve for your actions. Your illness may have been chosen as a vehicle of enlightenment. Your illness may provide an example to your family members. There are various reasons why you may be suffering physically. Accept it as a path towards spiritual growth.

There once lived a saint by the name of Bayazid. He used to say, "I never pray to God to give me anything.

Whatever I deserve in the eyes of God will be given to me. Whatever is harmful to me, God will keep away from me. I will leave everything in the hands of God." There came a time when Bayazid was hungry, poor, and without shelter. He sat by a tree at night in a dangerous area. His disciple asked, "Is God aware of your situation right now? You are starving, with no food and no shelter. Nobody is offering you any help. Are you sure that God is aware that his Sufi saint is suffering so much?" Bayazid replied, "God knows that this is exactly what I need in this situation. God knows when to give us poverty and when to give us food. This is what God is giving me at this particular time; I must accept it."

There are thousands of angels surrounding us every minute of our lives. We cannot see them, but they are here, witnessing our daily events. They watch us grow through suffering. They constantly guide our subconscious. They make us more spiritual beings.

Suffering comes in many forms. Accept it, learn from it, and grow because of it. Suffering makes us stronger, wiser and more courageous. Play your role as father, mother, sister, brother, and friend. Accept each consequence of suffering with open arms and yield to the path of spiritual growth.

A Little Forgiveness goes a Long Way

If you are looking for a way to encourage your spiritual growth dramatically, God has given your soul an instrument to do so. It is called forgiveness. Sooner or later, we have to learn to forgive.

There are many aspects of forgiveness. You have to ask for forgiveness from God, and you have to seek forgiveness from those people whom you have mistreated. Once you ask forgiveness, you will also have to learn to return it. You must forgive others for their mistreatment of you.

There are certain acts which God can forgive. Wrongdoing which does not involve another human being can be forgiven by the mercy of God. For example, if you have deliberately polluted earth or inflicted pain on God's creatures, you will have to seek for forgiveness from God. If you have inflicted pain on human beings, however, God may not forgive you on their behalf. You will have to seek forgiveness from the person whom you mistreated, in this life or the next.

The wheel of karma turns forever. The law of karma states that every action has a consequence. One way to escape from this tedious cycle of cause and effect, birth and death, is to use the power of forgiveness. You are not aware of every wrongdoing that requires forgiveness.

Your negative acts, like all aspects of your past lives, are locked in the subconscious mind. God is very compassionate. He knows that you are not aware of your past mistakes. He will give you many opportunities to seek forgiveness and, more importantly, to grant forgiveness.

Your family members, your friends, and your colleagues are around you because you have to forgive them. In today's society, we hear of many situations dealing with child abuse, being unfaithful to your marriage partner, children abusing their parents and so on. A person you may not know may suddenly appear in front of you and insult you for no apparent reason.

The only way to get out of this destructive cycle of pain and retaliation is to learn to forgive. First you must accept and forgive all the harm that has been done to you. Then you must steer your free will in the right direction.

Once you have forgiven, move on. Do not continue the cycle by responding angrily to the individual who mistreated you.

Psychotherapy has become very popular. This treatment deals with psychological disturbances that conventional medicine cannot successfully treat. Psychotherapists who use regression therapy to heal agree that many symptoms are the result of early emotional trauma. They also believe that the original suffering may have come from past lives. These traumas later manifest themselves as cancer, depression, neurosis, arthritis, loss of appetite, or various other illnesses.

Psychotherapists often tell their patients that they need to forgive a particular person or group in order to heal themselves. Quite often, the illness begins to disappear once the patient forgives and lets go. From a spiritual point of view, this therapy makes sense and is very helpful in treating the patient.

The therapist may have to regress the patient far into the past to discover the incident that caused the trauma. The patient has repressed the memory. Even though the patient seems unaware of the trauma, it is a part of a deep, subconscious memory, and it causes serious physical and mental damage. When you forgive, then, you have to do so from the depth of your soul. Making the motions of forgiveness does not mean that you have truly forgiven. Forgiving is not as easy as it sounds. You have to go consciously into the depths of your soul to be able to forgive. This is why you sometimes need the help of a psychotherapist.

An individual you knew in a past life, thousands of years ago, may come in contact with you. This individual may redress past karma with you in the form of forgiveness. You may not be aware of who this person is, but your subconscious remembers from the past.

Usually, the person who forgives benefits more than the person who is forgiven. Sometimes when you come into contact with a certain person, you experience an inexplicable antipathy. This person may have harmed you in the past; God is giving you a chance either to forgive this person or to compound the injury. At this point, you will have to use your wisdom; you will have to forgive and move on. This will be one of the most difficult decisions you will make because your natural tendency will be to retaliate.

You have to learn to forgive first and then forget. How can you forget first and then forgive? By forgetting, you will not know what it is that you have to forgive. The only way to move forward in your journey is to break the ties that connect you to the past. The only way to break them is by consciously forgiving. Get into the habit of asking for forgiveness from God and those around you. More importantly, get into the habit of forgiving others. You will be many levels closer to enlightenment, once you learn how to forgive.

The Power of Silence

In order for us to survive in this world, we are forced to use words to communicate with others. In our early years, we learn the alphabet and, then to read and write. While going through school, while communicating with our friends and family, and while earning a living, we must use speech. From the time we are born, we are discouraged from experiencing the dimension of silence. It seems that language is the key element that makes us human, and without it, we cannot be a part of the human society.

Just as the body and brain need rest, the soul needs an opportunity to unwind. Language is the result of the intellect urging the mouth to speak. The intellect is the nucleus of the body. The brain gives commands to the physical body, but the brain is entirely controlled by the soul. Silence not only benefits the body and the mind, but also the soul.

In today's society, noise pollution is increasing by the minute. We cannot escape noise from work, computers, televisions, radios, and transportation vehicles. Each noise produces its own sound frequencies, and the cumulative effect is difficult to calculate. Scientists are doing extensive research in this field.

Mahavira, a great master of ancient times, did not use any language for twelve years. He remained completely silent, in a state of meditation. When he spoke, the words came from the divine soul. These silent words of Mahavira brought his disciples enlightenment. Learning to practice silence enables us to approach the spiritual world.

When all thoughts cease, spiritual experience takes place. Jesus Christ said, "The kingdom of God is within you." The only way to get a glimpse of this kingdom is to go silently inside yourself. You cannot approach this kingdom busily talking. You must let go of all thoughts and words first.

A divine prayer is just silence. In silence, all the distractions around you disappear. When doing nothing, your ego disappears, your problems disappear, your worries become non-existent. In silence, you become one with the self.

If you are sitting quietly without uttering a single word but a thousand thoughts are rushing through your head, you are not experiencing silence. There are noises inside you: your work reproaching you, your family members making claims, money slipping away, your bills hounding you. Silence means to let go of all these burdens.

On behalf of your soul, make a point of finding half an hour a day to sit in silence. This simple therapy will benefit your soul tremendously. Make yourself a hot cup of tea and find yourself an empty place in your house. For half an hour, remove yourself from your family, your work, your pressures, and sit comfortably in silence. Silence benefits all three components of the human being: the body, the mind, and the soul.

We are now living in the space age. Science, technology, and information are rapidly evolving at a tremendous pace. Times have changed, values have changed, and society has changed. In earlier times, people were naturally inclined towards silence and meditation. They performed meditation for several hours a day. More time was spent with nature. There was more time to contemplate. With the increasing demands in our society, just half an hour of silence will make a significant difference in our lives.

Silence should be a fundamental part of your daily schedule. Studies show that individuals with high-pressure jobs have a greater chance of committing suicide. There has to be a spiritual way to release your everyday tension. Silence is the answer.

When one engages in silence, a special meeting takes place; a union occurs. You simply dissolve. It is like the ice melting away into the air when the sun rises. When silence arises, the frozen ego starts melting. Suddenly the ocean is there, the ego is gone.

When we go to sleep for eight hours, we do not experience silence. We are usually woken several times by external or internal disturbances. When we are sleeping, we are in an unconscious state. But when we go into silence, we are consciously going into silence. There is a very fine line between the two, but they are worlds apart. Insomnia is one the greatest complaints of our society. Try practicing silence for half an hour before sleeping and you will be surprised at the results.

Spirituality is born within you; religion takes place within you. The reason you go to the outer temple is so you can find the inner temple one day. You must take a trip inside of yourself and rediscover what was already there. When you are in silence, you will feel a great illumination spreading out from the heart.

We all carry the seed within us. We must encourage the seed to open. The only way to nurture this seed is to sprinkle it with the water of silence. Silence is power, silence is meditation, silence is growth, and silence is the key to enlightenment.

The Art of Witnessing

Life has become a repetitive mechanical process. We follow the same sequence of activities day in and day out. We behave like robots, not humans. The pressures of society have moulded our behaviour to an invariable pattern. The same song keeps playing until finally the record breaks down.

The art of witnessing is a spiritual method devised by the ancient sages to help create awareness of the soul.

Buddha mastered the technique of witnessing. To be a witness, you simply have to become an observer of activities. Just watch. Do not judge; do not become emotionally involved.

Life is very beautiful, precious, and magical. Every second, thousands of miracles are taking place all around us. Since our inner eyes are shut, we remain oblivious. When we pass by a flower, we do not realize its beauty. Stop for a moment and fix your attention on the flower. Don't look at the flower with preconceptions; don't judge the flower. Just become one with the flower. You will experience oneness with the beauty of the flower.

From now on, resist the impulse to perform your tasks in the usual mechanical manner. Do them as a witness. All you have to do is witness the event. If you have to play a role in the daily events, play your role but observe yourself.

When you wash your face in the morning, look at yourself in the mirror and remind yourself, "Today, I will only witness events. I will witness my role as a parent; I will witness my role as an employee; I will witness my role as a child; I will witness all my activities of the day."

When you see your children in the morning, remind yourself that these children are not really yours. They are simply passengers on the same journey. They are also individual souls who have come to earth for a short time. Fulfill your responsibilities to them, but as a witness. When they go to school, don't worry about them. Transfer the focus of your observation to the next event.

When talking to your marriage partner, remind yourself that your partner is a temporary companion; you will not be together forever. Give your partner a chance to perform necessary duties. Look at your partner's gestures; observe various moods and reactions. Watch your partner with complete attention. But don't interfere with your partner's actions; you are there only as a witness.

When you arrive at work, recognize that your fellow employees are individual spirits trying to make professional decisions in order to survive. Look at their different reactions when they are confronted with their daily tasks. Once again keep your emotions in check; eliminate your usual bias; don't judge anyone. Don't interfere with their actions. Speak only when you have to and, even then, speak as a witness.

On the way home, calmly observe all the drivers around you. Don't drive angrily or impatiently; you will no longer be a witness. Remind yourself that we are all temporary drivers on a road towards eternity. We are all spiritual brothers and sisters going towards the same destination.

When you start observing others you will be able to see your common mistakes clearly. By observing an event with your inner eyes, you can correct your own behaviour towards others. By witnessing the events at work, you will not make the same mistakes as your co-workers. You will be a better employee and a better human being. You will be a better parent, because you made the effort of witnessing your children's behaviour. By witnessing your partner's actions, you will know how to avoid conflicts. You will be a better marriage partner.

Witnessing is a constant process of consciousness. When you drive, drive consciously; when you work, do it consciously. When you are a parent, be a conscious parent. The art of witnessing simply keeps you aware at all times. As you become more aware, you will cease to be prey to your emotions. The more conscious you are, the less you will judge. The more you witness, the fewer mistakes you will make.

The law of karma says, "Every action causes a reaction." By becoming a witness, you immediately become aware of each action you instigate. Your daily activities become a form of meditation for you. You are not giving your emotions or ego a chance to react, since awareness is controlling your actions.

We must also learn to witness our own absent-mindedness. Note all the thoughts that pass through your mind. Memories are aroused; anger, sadness, and bliss succeed each other. Witness all these thoughts passing through one by one. Let all the thoughts merge into your consciousness. The mind is like a crowded highway; as soon as one car passes the next one comes. Let them all keep coming. After a while, the highway of thoughts will start to slow down. So no matter what activity takes place during your day, witness that activity, become aware of it. Let that moment move you towards consciousness.

The art of witnessing is a form of meditation that you can perform throughout the day. It helps your spirit evolve to a higher level. This simple technique can give you access to the soul if you learn to use it in the right way. Take this art seriously and you will see the benefits.

Total Surrender

Surrender yourself completely to the divine. Whatever occurs in your life is through the compassion of the Almighty. Submit every aspect of your life to God. Your wealth, health, family, prosperity, and success are all the result of God's compassion.

You have heard the saying, "Struggle is the meaning of life; victory or defeat is in the hands of God." Struggle with your job, struggle with your health, struggle to provide for your family, struggle to keep a balance between the temporal and the spiritual, but leave the outcome to God. God knows best when to respond and when not to respond. God knows how to respond and how not to respond.

Our understanding of victory and defeat is not the same as God's. What we consider victories with our limited understanding may be defeats when viewed from a larger perspective. Achievements of the material world are quite different from those of the spiritual world. Spiritual logic is a totally different dimension than everyday logic.

God cannot be conquered. Such a goal is misguided and it is like saying that the fish wants to conquer the mighty ocean. We have to be conquered by God. We need to have a desire for God to conquer our soul. The mind is very aggressive; it wants to conquer the world, and own it. This attitude is not appropriate to a spiritual search. The only way to appease God is to surrender yourself. Surrender your ego, surrender your aggression, and surrender your strategies. Become humble and surrender yourself.

You must open the doors of your heart and invite God to come inside. Don't demand God's presence. You must prepare the necessary ground to welcome God. Make sure that the ground in your heart is fertile. Make sure that the soil is rich and full of nutrients. Sprinkle it with the water of total surrender. As soon as God sees that your heart is fertile and rich, He will plant the seed of enlightenment. From this seed will bloom a thousand-petalled lotus within your heart. Then your heart will be the palace of God.

Modern society forces us to be aggressive in all aspects of our lives. We are aggressive with our education; we want to be better informed than our neighbours. We are aggressive with our jobs since others are waiting for the opportunity to take them. We are aggressive with our bank accounts; we want high interest savings. We are aggressive with our family members; we must establish our authority. We live in an atmosphere of aggression.

Put your fears and aggression to rest. All the prominent scriptures in this world maintain that the material benefits you deserve will definitely come to you. Nature will provide for your needs. Don't be tied to this world because of your insecurities. Go to work, gain an honest living, and leave the rest to God. What is yours will always come to you.

Since most of our actions have aggressive intentions, we tend to use the same behaviour with God. This kind of behaviour will not work in the spiritual world. Learn to be humble in the presence of God. You must become passive and let God be the aggressor.

A politician has to follow the same path of humility when searching for God. In God's presence the rules of political power do not apply. A scientist must submit his soul to God. God is not an object that can be measured, nor is He an equation that you can produce through a given set of formulae. A philosopher will also have to let go of his preconceived ideas in the presence of God. If you wish to surrender to God, do so by abandoning your material of aggression. There is nothing wrong in being a politician, a scientist, or a philosopher. By all means, be the best you can be. What has to be understood here is that you cannot apply the rules of your everyday lives when you are seeking the unknown. All ideologies of your profession must be put aside when seeking the higher entity.

The mind will not be able to understand what worship is. It will have to surrender first. Spiritual people surrender first; they pray, they are patient, they open the doors of their heart. They put their faith in God. They say to God, "This is your kingdom. Come when you please. We await your presence." This is the attitude of those on the path of spirituality. When God sees a house that is ready to be occupied, He enters instantly.

Accept everything that revolves around your daily life. If there is a problem with your health, have the courage to accept your illness. If you have a loved one who is suffering and it is beyond your power to help him, simply accept it. If you have lost a loved one, try to accept it. If you are suffering from poverty, try to accept it.

Although it is very difficult to accept calamities, despondency moves you away from God. Each individual faces an unfortunate situation at some point. Physically we feel tormented; emotionally we suffer deeply. However, you must remember that the first step towards the Almighty is a total surrender to your circumstances. Completely accept what existence has given to you. By accepting your misfortunes you are showing courage to God. This courage is a necessary requisite in spiritual growth. Believe it or not, this courage is only a small token of the courage you will require to be in the presence of God.

We all come to earth to learn, through the body, mind, and soul. One of the most difficult lessons we have to learn is how to surrender to the divine. Surrender happens in phases. It is not possible to surrender all at once. It happens in stages during our lifetimes; we are placed in situations that require surrender.

The whole idea is to surrender willingly to God. This is very difficult to do. Normally, we are forced to surrender to a certain situation. When we lose a loved one, we are not willing to let go. We go into denial. After a while, we realize that the person is not coming back and we pray to God, "I am surrendering to you. Please take care of my loved one, wherever he is."

The same thing happens with other aspects of our life. Money comes and goes, health comes and goes, relationships come and go, family members come and go. All this is really a game. Learn to play it well. The only way to play this game is to surrender to God totally. Leave everything to him: your health, wealth, family, and soul.

Love: The Key Ingredient

We come to earth to experience the different facets of love. The entire universe revolves around various forms of love. The more affection we bring to existence, the more we will receive. Love starts in a physical realm and then blossoms into a spiritual realm. Before we can experience the spiritual bliss of God, we must experience love on a smaller, human scale.

Before we begin to give our affection to others, we are given the opportunity to receive love. From the moment we are born, we receive love. On the first day of our life, our entire family is present to celebrate our arrival. The baby can feel all the love coming from every member of the family. The body of the baby may be small, but the soul is fully aware of its surroundings.

In the first few years of infancy, the baby is bathed in the mother's limitless love. The mother reaches into the depths of her soul and provides immense love for her child. The mother gives love and the baby receives it. Every cell of the growing child seeks love from the mother. Psychologists claim that whatever children are given in their formative years will be the basis of their future life. The way a child matures depends entirely on the formative years.

Recent scientific studies indicate that you will become the same kind of parent as your own parents. If you grew up in an environment full of love, you will also provide immense love for your child. If your childhood lacked affection, you may not be as giving as an adult.

There are different forms of love that one can experience. Each form helps us grow in different ways. We will experience love as parents, children, friends, and companions. Existence has provided us with animals, the outdoors, plants, and nature to love.

As we grow, the quality of our love slowly matures. We feel a special type of love towards our mother and father. We begin to follow the rules and principles set out by our parents. When we communicate with elderly grandparents, we feel a different bond with them. It is said that the bond between a grandparent and a grandchild is even stronger than the bond between a parent and a child. As adolescents, we spend most of our time with our friends. Friendship offers a different type of love. We would do anything to help or protect our best friends. We will encounter many situations in the company of our best friends and we will learn from them.

As you approach adulthood, you learn how to give love, rather than simply receive it. You were surrounded by the love of your parents, grandparents and friends. Soon it will be time for you to become a parent. You will shower your children with the same kind of love that you once received. You have been given an opportunity to receive love as a child and give love as an adult. These two prerequisites have to be fulfilled before you are ready to cultivate spiritual love toward the divine.

It has been proven that when you give love to plants, they respond in a very positive way. When individuals talk or sing to plants, the plants are happy. When you avoid them, they do not flourish. Even plants need love and nurturing.

A house pet can be as close to you as a family member. Whether it is a dog, a cat, or a budgie, it also requires love. Have you ever considered why God has given you a pet? It is to help you expand your capacity for love.

Existence gives you many opportunities to share love. Extend your love to areas beyond your immediate family. When you go out for a walk, share your love with the flowers around you. Be compassionate to the trees around you. Smile at the grass you walk on. Remember that flowers, plants, trees, animals, and nature in general have souls. Those souls are alive and breathing.

Up to this point, we have discussed love in its material form. The love you have for your parents, children, friends, animals and nature is a material form of love. Now you must focus your love on the spiritual dimension. This dimension is hidden, esoteric, and unknown. Love for God is the ultimate form of love.

Love of God should be unconditional, unbiased, and unlimited. Love will give you inner strength. Love will give you integrity. Love is the preparation for enlightenment. You have been taught to love for many lifetimes.

Before the flower of spiritual love blooms, all the seedlings of material love have to bloom. The seedlings are the love you have experienced as a child, a parent, a grandparent, friend, and caretaker. Now focus on the spiritual dimension. It is time for the eternal flower of love to blossom. The flower of spiritual love is located in the heart. The only way it will bloom is if you sprinkle it with the water of meditation. Meditation is a form of spiritual love. Through meditation, your love for the Almighty will grow day by day. We have traveled far and long to experience all the early stages of love. Now it is time to experience the advanced form of love. The time has come to experience the ultimate secret of God, spiritual love. This love awaits you in the heart. Seek the love of God in your heart.

Love every aspect of this universe. Expand your love to its utmost capacity. Love your neighbour, your family, your pet, your friends, and most of all, your soul. Love for your spirit is the ultimate form of love. The only way to love your soul is to spend time with it. The more you love your spirit, the more you love God. Spiritual love is the most profound form of love you will experience as a human being.

Temporal and Spiritual

Throughout history, humanity has been provided with saints and sages who shed light on spiritual matters. We have been constantly reminded by divinely inspired souls to keep a balance in our lives, a balance between the world of spirit and the world of matter. We must seek to make the most of both worlds: the material world, which we live in from day to day, and the spiritual world, which is often obscure to us.

In our daily lives, there are many challenges that we must encounter. We have a responsibility to educate ourselves, look after our physical bodies, provide for our families, and survive in this world. During the daytime, close to one hundred percent of our time is spent in material-related areas. From the time we get up in the morning until we come home in the evening, our energy is dissipated in worldly activities. Very little attention is given to our souls, the spiritual dimension.

We all come to earth to fulfill a great number of tasks. We have a responsibility towards the material world and we have to fulfill it. It is misleading to pretend otherwise. There is absolutely nothing wrong in meeting the challenges that confront us in our daily lives. Be the best that you can possibly be - the best parent, the best child, the best employee, the best athlete, and the best student.

However, don't forget the fact that you have a soul that needs nurturing. In order for you to be able to keep up with your daily worldly activities, you have to learn to receive guidance from your soul. There are three elements in a human: body, mind, and soul. All three must be encouraged.

In today's society, a lot of attention is given to our physical bodies. Fitness centers have proliferated in the last few years. They give us all kinds of tools to improve our health, stamina, and life expectancy. People are improving their diets and watching their cholesterol levels. They are focusing on low-fat and high-fiber diets. Anti-oxidant nutrients are recommended as a defense against diseases. We even are willing to try holistic medicine to help the body. The human body is the temple of God and we must take proper care of it.

The material world has advanced tremendously in the last few centuries. There have been great achievements in the fields of science, medicine, technology, and communications. In Western countries, information and technology are often obsolete within a few years. In order to survive, we are becoming more competitive than ever before.

A bachelor's degree no longer guarantees a good job. Students must diversify their areas of study in order to join the workforce. Individuals are spending many years of their lives in academic institutions; students are graduating with master degrees in one field and PhD's in another. Even when you have a career, your information has to be continually updated in order to survive. The human intellect is pushed beyond its limits.

We are paying attention to two of the three elements of human life: the body is striving to be in better shape and the mind is getting a tremendous workout. But, what happens to our soul? We must start giving it serious attention. Our bodies are temporal; our minds are temporal. Our souls, however, are eternal; the soul is the most precious element of a human being.

Realize that your soul is of the utmost importance. If your body and mind do not retain a balance with your spirit, you will eventually burn out. There will be no peace within you. The knowledge you gain from academic institutions is necessary for material survival, but the knowledge of the soul is an entirely different matter. Focus on the world of spirituality; keep a balance.

There is no need to renounce the world. There is no need to run away to a monastery. There is no need to travel to the Himalayas to search for God. God is inside of you; look for God within yourself. Remain in the world without becoming attached to it. The person who faces the world, accepts its challenges, and yet communicates with the soul is the real mystic. A mystic is not one who runs away from responsibilities and hides in the mountains.

Live in this world and create a Himalaya inside of your heart. Become silent in the noise. Remain in your house and yet be a mystic. The way of renunciation is that of the fearful. So be in the world, but don't let the world be in you. By living in this world, you are fulfilling your karma. You are showing courage by accepting your responsibilities. If you run away, you will have to come back to fulfill your destiny. We can run but we cannot hide from God. So be a part of this world and also be a part of your soul.

Love, but don't lose yourself to love. Become a part of your family and yet remain separate from them. Remain sincere to both your responsibilities and your soul. Go for your daily workouts, but also exercise the spirit. If you keep reminding yourself of the spirit, eventually you will not need to remember the spirit - the spirit will remember you.

Live in this world fully; make the most of it. Make the most of your body, make the most of your mind, and, above all, make the most of your soul. Live in complete balance and harmony. Physically, mentally, and spiritually, be the best you can be.

Loneliness and Aloneness

Loneliness and aloneness are opposites. Loneliness is a negative state of mind; aloneness is positive. One leads you to misery and depression. The other leads you to bliss, eternal freedom, and enlightenment.

Fear and insecurities manifest themselves in the form of loneliness. We constantly rely on others to keep us entertained. Loneliness is very harmful to our soul. Until we are able to transform loneliness into aloneness, we will depend on the material world to fill the gap of loneliness.

To be lonely means to miss the presence of another. We may miss our friends, our family, our job, or even some form of entertainment. The mind requires constant occupation. It is afraid of even a fleeting sense of emptiness.

The fear of having nothing to do is so profound that we schedule our activities several weeks in advance. Before the weekend arrives, we plan each moment so we won't be in the unfortunate position of having nothing to do.

When we have nothing to do, we say that we are bored. When there is no activity, we enter a state of passivity. This state of non-doing is necessary in the early stages of meditation. Life has taught us to be very aggressive. We live in a highly competitive society; our natural instincts are to be aggressive.

We aggressively pursue our academic education, our job, and money. We must be the masters of our destiny. As long as the mind follows the habits of aggression, it will remain in a state of loneliness. We must let go of our egotistical way of life and learn to be a little more passive. We have forgotten the fact that the divine controls the laws of the universe. It is our job to be responsible and make an effort. The fruits of that effort, however, are in the hands of God.

There are many people who have lost vast amounts of money. There are also those who go from rags to riches. Why does this happen? Whatever material situation is best for you will come to you without delay. There is no need to be overly aggressive.

In order to transform loneliness into aloneness, we must balance our ratio of aggression to passivity. Generally aggression is much more common than passivity. To make this transformation, you will have to learn to control aggressive tendencies.

The only way to become more passive is to meditate. You must be alone in order to meditate properly. You could be quietly sitting in a room, a garden or prayer house away from all your worldly activity. Why do you have to be apart from material activity? The primary reason is to experience aloneness. You must be away from your family members, job, money, TV set, and the rest of the world. You must be completely alone.

In a state of meditation, your mind is at complete rest. You are not working, driving, listening to music, or distracted by your family members. You are completely alone with your soul. This non-activity takes you from loneliness to aloneness, from aggression to non-aggression.

During the first few stages of aloneness, you will feel bored and uncomfortable. Your mind is used to clinging to the material world. For many lifetimes, your mind has resisted the state of aloneness. It will rebel like a wild animal that has been caged for the first time. Unleash all the repressed energies. The house inside your mind needs cleaning. There is dust everywhere. No light can filter through the windows. When you initially clean a neglected house, the dust particles fill the air. Air the house; get rid of the refuse that your mind has collected. Make yourself completely empty.

The more time you spend in a state of in aloneness, the closer you will come to the divine. We must learn to act in a civilized manner when approaching the presence of God. Our habitual aggressive tactics will not work.

The more we meditate, the less lonely we will feel. The more we become attached to the Creator, the less we miss our old addictions. If you must cling to someone, let it be your Creator. The more you are alone, the closer you come to the divine spirit in your heart.

Older individuals seem to be increasingly comfortable with aloneness. Grandparents have gone through the responsible stages of life. They have finished working, and raising and providing for their family. Now there is nothing more to do. Now is the time to be alone. We often go to our elders because they seem to be wise. In the late stages of life, they can look back at the events and learn from them. They can teach youth how to avoid mistakes.

Since older people do not have much to do, they have time to ponder spiritual concepts. They often think about their Creator and the purpose of their journey. Older individuals seem to be particularly innocent because they have experienced aloneness. It is said that your senior years are like a second childhood. An infant is pure and innocent. A child is also in a state of aloneness in the early years. This innocence and purity flowers for the second time in the senior years.

As much as possible, practice aloneness. Spend as much time with yourself as possible. In aloneness, your innocence and purity will return, and you will approach the divine.

Different Levels of the Soul

Different Levels of the Soul

Every human being who comes to earth must go through the gradual process of going from childhood to adulthood. Similarly, our souls must go through an evolutionary growth from infancy to full spiritual maturity. Some of us have been traveling for a long time, and some of us are still young.

People like to be with their peers. Infants like to be around other children of their own age. The elderly like the

95

company of older and more mature individuals. Those in between tend to seek out their own age group.

As the soul starts to grow, its level of wisdom, compassion, understanding, and love increases. We begin to view the world from a different perspective. The older we get, the closer we come to the spiritual dimension. We move away from youthful ideas and closer to ancient wisdom.

When you come into contact with others, don't be content with purely external communication. Look deep into the soul of the other person. Look deep into the spirit within the human body. When you try to communicate with another's spiritual aspect, you are learning to see with the eyes of your soul.

Suddenly, you will pick up subtle vibrations from the people around you. These vibrations can be interpreted by the inner eyes of your soul. You will immediately be attracted or repelled. The vibrations can be filled with warmth, love, and compassion or they can convey anger, hate, and negativity.

If the vibrations from the people around you are similar to your own, you will naturally respond to them. If not, you will recoil. We can have lifelong affection for best friends, relatives and colleagues. The compatibility of the souls is so strong that there is never a conflict. With others, conflicts arise quickly; your paths begin to separate.

The more the soul grows, the more intense the spirit becomes. The older it gets, the more concentrated the inner light will become. The wiser it gets, the more it will pursue other old souls.

When we are young, we turn to our elders for support. Mother and father provide constant support and love.   Similarly, all souls that are spiritually young turn to older spirits for support and guidance. Younger souls often come into contact with an older soul just to experience their vibrations. There are always a few adult souls to supervise the young souls playing with their friends.

Contemplate this story.   There once lived a great emperor named Akbar. He had nine wise men in his council to guide him. These men were called the nine jewels of the emperor. Once, Akbar turned to his wise men in a rage, and said, "Everyone claims that you are the wisest men in the world and yet I have not learned anything from you. You have never displayed your wisdom to me!" At this point, a child entered the palace. He wanted to see Akbar and his kingdom. As soon as the child saw Akbar, he began to laugh. Akbar said, "Why are you laughing? Didn't your father teach you that it is bad manners to laugh in the royal court?" The child replied, "I am laughing because I know why you have not been able to benefit from your wise men."

The great emperor was puzzled, looked deep into the eyes of the child, and asked, "Can you enlighten me?" The child said, "You will have to get off your throne first and let me sit on it." Akbar rose; the child sat on the throne and the emperor sat at his feet. The child said, "Now ask me for wisdom." Akbar understood, and a transformation took place inside of him. He touched the feet of the child and said, "Just by sitting at your feet, I have been transformed by your wisdom. I do not need to ask you anything; you have already given so much." We can learn so much from this story. Who is the real king and who is the child? Royalty should be measured by the wisdom of a soul, not by physical age or wealth.

An old soul may take the form of a child, friend, parent or teacher. There are many young souls and few old ones. It is like a kindergarten classroom full of children playing, with only a few teachers to keep an eye on them.

The older the soul gets, the more it tires of the material world. The desire to connect with the outside world weakens. Youngsters have more energy to play and socialize. The elderly minimize their worldly activities. It takes more effort to accomplish the things that were so easy to achieve in youth. We played our games in our youth. Now it is time to surrender to the inner reality. The soul has been on a long journey; it is time to retire to the divine.

After traveling for many lifetimes, the spirit within us becomes old. It is probable that the ancient sages were old souls. Their guidance, sermons, and knowledge show the wisdom of innumerable years.

We must all go from childhood to old age. Step by step, we rise higher and higher until, finally, we are ready to join the universal consciousness.

Growth of the Soul

Each lifetime contributes to our maturity and rich variety of experience. Each individual journey that we make on earth takes us to a higher level of evolution. Although the aim of meditation is not to take you into the past, you must acknowledge that you have evolved through many lives to come to the present point. In order for you to achieve enlightenment, you must focus on the present.

All of us must experience the various aspects of spiritual growth. We mature through our experiences of motherhood, fatherhood, childhood, poverty, wealth, illness, and relationships.

An individual who has experienced a multi-dimensional life is ready to bloom into divine consciousness. Your free will is given the opportunity to make a series of choices. If you make the wrong choice, then you will have a chance to correct it in the future. Your education simply takes a little longer. The only way you will learn is if you have been given a chance to experience all aspects of growth.

Let us contemplate a story of Buddha. When Buddha was born, his father was approached by an astrologer. He was told, "Your son has the potential to choose one of two paths. Either he will become one of the world's greatest emperors or he will become a mystic." Buddha's father asked, "How is it possible to face such an extreme choice? I am confused. Please explain this to me." The astrologer said, "It is said in the scriptures that when a very wealthy individual suddenly has a spiritual awakening, he divests himself of all material wealth. This may be the case with Buddha."

Buddha's father became worried and looked for ways to ensure that his son would succeed him. He said to his astrologers, "I have only one son. I am very old. My wife passed away immediately after she gave birth to Buddha, so I cannot have any more sons. The future of my kingdom is jeopardized. Please help me." The astrologers made predictions that were based on their books. They said, "Under no circumstances, should you allow Buddha to experience any pain, misery, or sadness. Make sure you keep him away from the elderly and shield him from the idea of death. Surround him with beautiful women. Let him live a life of luxury, happiness, and comfort."

Buddha's father followed the advice of his astrologers. Three mansions were built for Buddha. In the summer, he lived in a cool house. As the seasons changed, he would move to his other homes. Buddha was surrounded by beautiful women, wealth, and luxury. It was said that not even a flower was allowed to die in the palace of Buddha. As soon as a flower faded, it was immediately removed. One night Buddha was being entertained. There were beautiful girls dancing, music and laughter; suddenly, he fell asleep. He woke up in the middle of the night. The girls had gone to sleep and one was having a nightmare.

For once Buddha's eyes did not rest on beauty. He actually felt repelled by the women. He experienced reality but kept silent. Later, on his way to a festival, Buddha saw an old man. He asked his chariot driver, "What has happened to this man? Why does he look so wrinkled and decrepit?" The driver said, "It happens to everybody. We all become frail as we grow old." Buddha's chariot passed a funeral procession. He asked his driver, "What has happened to this other man? Why are people carrying him on their shoulders?" The driver said, "The man is dead, sir. We must all die eventually." Buddha said, "Stop this chariot. Will I also die one day?"

The driver knew that Buddha's father had tried to protect his son from the idea of death. However, he was honest and told Buddha, "We all have to die one day. Whoever takes birth must also die." Shortly after, a monk appeared behind the dead man. Buddha asked, "Who is this man? Why is he wearing a robe?" The driver answered, "This man has renounced life and is in search of the essence." Buddha said, "I have renounced it as well." By nightfall, Buddha had left the palace.

Buddha had the opportunity to live with material wealth. He experienced riches, luxury, and royal esteem. It is no accident that Buddha was born to royalty. Buddha had to experience wealth. Only after this experience was he ready to choose the other extreme. If Buddha had been born a beggar, it is quite possible that he would have wished to become a king. This would have hindered his spiritual growth. God gave him a chance to fulfill his desire and cleared his path for enlightenment.

When we take birth, we come with a long list of desires. These desires are fulfilled one at a time. We all have desires such as wealth, health, power, and control. We want to be a political leader, a doctor, a lawyer, a nurse, a father, a mother, and so on. There are two ways of fulfilling desires. One way is to experience the desire and the other way is to relinquish it. The latter method is much more difficult. It requires great concentration and meditation. God measures your ability to relinquish your desire. If the only way to fulfill a particular desire is to experience it, existence will give you a chance to experience it, as long as it does not harm your soul. On the other hand, if you practice meditation, and relinquish your desire, you will experience tremendous spiritual growth.

There are repressed desires from our past lives locked into our subconscious. We are not aware of our past lives, nor are we aware of our repressed desires. This is why we encounter so many experiences in our lifetime. Some experiences are happy, and some, sad. Some seem enjoyable, and some, tedious. One of the primary reasons we keep coming back to earth is to fulfill our long list of desires. God is very compassionate: the more things you ask for, the more you will get. However, it will take you longer to achieve spiritual enlightenment.

If you can learn the secret of following your heart, you will eliminate many of your old, deep, and distracting desires. Desires are a part of your mind. Let go of the mind, and you immediately let go of your desires. Just as gravity naturally pulls you down, the heart, which is the palace of God, is naturally pulling your soul down to enlightenment. Do yourself a favour, follow your heart.

In order for us to reach our full spiritual potential, we must go through every experience, from one extreme to the other. All stones must be turned. This is one reason that some people suffer in poverty, while others enjoy a life of luxury. Some are healthy; some are ill. Some die early, and some die late. Some are males, and some are females. All these examples are pieces of the same puzzle. When all the pieces are combined, you end up with a large, clear picture of the spiritual enlightenment.

The Law of Karma

Karma means actions. The law of karma is a universal system that is based on the concept of cause and effect. The law of physics states that every action produces an equal reaction. The law of karma works on the same principle. Positive karma encourages progress of the soul, and negative karma hinders the progress of the soul.

Karma can also mean the choices or decisions that one makes through free will. Throughout our lifetime, we are engaged in a series of choices. There are really only two options: either you make a positive choice or you make a negative choice. We are tested in a wide variety of contexts. We make choices involving our family situations, our physical bodies, our career, and so on. After a choice has been made, the results of that choice are apparent at various intervals. Many of the results will be witnessed in this lifetime; other outcomes will not be witnessed in this life. The laws of nature decide when and how you will witness the results of your actions.

Some choices we make affect us individually, but we also make choices that affect others. We are constantly making individual choices that affect our body, mind, and soul. For example, if you want to stay healthy, you have to eat properly and exercise regularly. In order to educate yourself, you must attend an academic institution. To benefit the soul, you must engage in religious activity and prayers. Every choice that you make which involves another individual directly affects your soul. When we make a decision that relates to another person, we do not immediately see its result. However, as soon as that action takes place, it is recorded. If, for example, you have secretly stolen some money from your best friend, the resulting negative karma will be recorded by your soul, by the soul of your friend, and by existence. Then existence will ensure that a situation will arise where this negative action is rectified. Likewise all actions cause similar reactions.

Many of the decisions we make are complex. They are rarely simple cases of right and wrong or white and black; there is a lot of gray area. If all decisions were simple, we would all be enlightened and the law of karma would cease to exist. What should be the basis of your decision when you are unsure of which way to go? The critical factor is your intentions. No matter what decision you make, if your intentions are good, you are heading in the right direction.

All souls in this world must rectify and learn from the choices they have made. Certain souls are given the opportunity to make choices that affect a large number of people. A political leader often makes decisions that affect millions of people. As a result, his karma is connected with every member of the country. The same idea applies to parents making decisions for their children, doctors for their patients, teachers for their students, a sage for his disciples, and so on. Some souls come down with a special purpose. Perhaps they have traveled for a long time to achieve the knowledge to make the right choices.

Let us assume you have a professional career, and you are making decisions that affect a large number of people. The individuals under your supervision will either prosper or suffer as a result of your actions. This situation is very common and often creates a dilemma. If you make an important decision for selfish reasons, your intentions are misleading you and everyone else. That one decision will affect many other individuals, and it will be permanently recorded by existence. On the other hand, if a decision is made with good intentions, even if there are more obstacles, your soul will immediately grow as a result of helping others.

Individuals often seek psychiatric treatment because of the guilt they feel. It comes from decisions they made earlier in their lifetime. Guilt is a cancer of the soul; it can destroy your spiritual health. If you know that you acted with good intentions, you will be able to let go of your guilt. Your soul will remind you that you based your decision on the best interests of other individuals; therefore, you have done all you can. Most situations you encounter should be dealt with in a similar manner.

The principles of karma do not apply to only one lifetime. It is an eternal system of debits and credits, an invisible bank account with multiple transactions. Let us now consider the eternal cycle of karma. What is predestination? What is free will? How do they relate to karma? All the circumstances that you encounter in this lifetime as a result of choices from past lives are predestined. All the choices you make in this lifetime from the time you are born are products of your free will. It is important for us to realize that both free will and predestination play a key role in the growth of our soul, and we must be open to both aspects.

The law of karma teaches us to accept the outcomes of our past actions. Our physical body, our parents, our children, our relationships, our health and wealth are all predestined. How we decide to handle our physical body, our parents, our children, our relationships, our health and wealth is a result of our free will.

The Vedas, among other prominent scriptures, shed light on this fundamental area. Vedic literature states that the soul is the spiritual element of the human that never dies. The soul is eternal. The soul lives in the body for a certain number of years and goes through a series of transformations. When the body is worn out, the soul departs and, after a short time, re-enters a mother's womb and assumes another body.

Psychologists now practice regression therapy. Patients are not only encouraged to return to their childhood, they can also go back to a previous lifetime. Quite often, a patient is given regression therapy to cure an illness that is untreatable by conventional medicine. All the illnesses that manifest themselves in the body, as well as those that affect the mind, are results of our past actions.

Between our physical eyes, in the center of our forehead, there is a third eye. The third eye is invisible to normal eyesight. It contains a blueprint, in minute detail, of each action of our present life and all our previous lives. The ancient sages of the East engaged in lengthy sessions of meditation. They could meditate for many hours without a break. They mastered the techniques of meditation to such an extent that they were able to approach the blueprint at will. They were able to read the blueprint page by page.

Each element in the universe revolves around a certain set of laws.

The body has a set of laws. If you eat too much, you become sick. If you sleep too much, you become lazy. If you don't exercise, your body starts to deteriorate. The soul also revolves around the laws of the spiritual world. It has to follow all the evolutionary stages, starting from life in the sea. The soul has a responsibility to keep a balance between the world of spirit and the world of matter.

Before a soul enters the womb of a mother, it chooses one mother and one father. Before the soul comes down, there are millions of potential mothers. Why does it choose that one particular mother? One of the main reasons is karma. A special bond was created between the mother and the child through a choice that was made in the past. The soul waits in the spirit world for the mother to be able to conceive. The link between the mother and the child continues for many lifetimes.

It is mentioned in the holy Gita (an ancient Indian scripture) that a mystic only chooses birth in the family of a mystic. The holy Gita teaches us that there has to be great compatibility between the soul that is taking birth and the parents who are giving birth. A mystic is a spiritually elevated soul whose karma is based on good or positive decisions. A soul with such an impressive record will only choose parents who also have spiritual qualities.

Family trees continue from one generation to another. It is possible for a great-grandfather to come back as a grandson. A family is a very special unit chosen by existence. Do not take the presence of your family members for granted. Your grandmother, your grandfather, father, mother, brothers, and sisters have been with you more times than you can imagine. Love them, help them, learn from them, and respect them. Build positive karma with them. You will need their help not only in this world but also in the spiritual world and other worlds.

Those who have had a near-death experience claim that when they are going towards the spiritual world, a deceased family member comes to receive them. They are absolutely correct. When we are in the spirit world, we have multi-sensory perception. We are aware of all our past lives. Family relationships continue in the spirit world. You should learn not to build any negative karma, especially with your loved ones. Jealousy, hate, tyranny, manipulation, and emotional abuse are all tools of negative karma. If one was to pass away after inflicting pain on his family members, he carries that burden of pain and guilt into the next world. He is then given another chance to return to this world and make things right.

According to the great epic the Mahabharata, journeying between this world and the spiritual world is an ongoing process. The disciple of Lord Krishna (a spiritual master) poses a very important question to the master. He asks the master if he had any past lives. Krishna explains to his disciple that he has evolved through many lives, but he was not aware of them. The concept of past lives was mentioned over 5000 years ago in this great epic. Today, many individuals are coming forward with experiences of life after death, near-death experiences, and experiences relating to reincarnation. All these concepts are linked to the law of karma.

Individuals who have had a near-death experience claim that there is one moment in particular that is very vivid. In an instant, every event that took place during their lifetime flashes before them. Good actions bring happiness and bad actions cause pain. All the events that we witness are the actions that were recorded in our personal blueprint, the diary of our daily lives. Clean up your diary and get rid of the blots on it. Start taking proper care of your soul by creating positive karma. Life after death and reincarnation have been assured in many Holy Scriptures. The more open you can be to esoteric concepts, the better your chances will be for spiritual growth.

When you decided to take birth, you came with a very large agenda to fulfill. In one lifetime, an individual endures much adversity, suffering, and pain. Ask an old man about all the events that took place during his lifetime and he will tell you volumes. Life will make all kinds of demands on you. It will ask for your money, services, love, happiness, health, and reputation.

So, you may be asking, how does all this benefit my soul? The answer is simple: it is not possible to attain spiritual union with God until all your debts are paid. So be wise and pay off as much as you can. There are many areas to consider in order for you to end the cycle of karma.

We are all individual souls on a journey towards the unknown. We don't own anyone or anything. Everything in this world is temporary. Even your physical body has been lent to you for a higher purpose. Every time you make a decision, make it consciously. Get into the habit of pausing a few seconds before making a decision. All decisions made out of anger, hate, and jealousy will hinder your progress. All decisions made out of love and awareness will enhance the quality of your soul.

During the course of a day, we are forced to make many decisions: decisions at work, decisions with our family members, decisions while driving, etc. In order to make you more conscious of the decisions you make on a daily basis, use the following technique. First you must always listen to your heart; that is where God resides. Any decision that does not involve another person, you can make immediately, as long as it does not harm your body, mind or soul. Any decision involving another person should be postponed for twenty-four hours if you feel at all unsure. After twenty-four hours, your decision will be made more calmly and consciously. Get into the habit of reminding yourself that your actions are interconnected with others around you.

Attachment and
Detachment

The world we live in has so much to offer us. When we're young we're given toys. It starts with a pretty doll or a cuddly teddy bear. As we get older, we get attached to different kinds of toys, toys for grown-ups.

We have a natural tendency to be attracted by tasty foods, fancy clothes, and flashy cars. We also tend to become overattached to our work. Different types of attachment are formed by each of our senses. Our eyes desire beauty and glamour. The mouth will pursue tasty foods and drinks. The nose likes to be surrounded by expensive flowers and delightful aromas. The ears love to hear music, gossip, and loud noises.

Every time our vision alights on an object of beauty, we yearn to possess it. Before we know it, our eyes are overwhelmed by beautiful objects, and we experience temporary blindness.

Our ears are always open to new issues. One of the most powerful influences on the ear is music. A scientific experiment was conducted by university students to see the effect of different types of music. In the first part of the experiment, heavy metal music was played in front of the plant. The plant actually started to move away from the tape recorder. In the second part of the experiment, Ravi Shankar's music was played. The plant came closer to the music and began to hug the tape recorder. Like plants, our souls also repel and embrace sound vibrations.

One of the most destructive sounds that your ears encounter is gossip. Gossip is Satan's tool; it can destroy your soul. If you engage in discussions about other people, be very careful; the best thing you can do on your soul's behalf is to close your ears. It is not possible to describe the damage done by gossip.

Scientists say that noise pollution is very high in today's society. Noises from television, radios, transportation vehicles, work, family and other pressures contribute to hearing loss, migraines, neurosis, and, ultimately, the destruction of the soul.

It is important to provide for your family. You must make sure that they are given food, shelter, and love. You must provide them with the best possible education. You must look after your parents and grandparents. This is a necessary part of fulfilling your promise to God. However, do not forget that in reality these children, these parents, and grandparents are not yours. Do not possess them; do not overwhelm them. Do not cling to them. They will not be with you forever. Provide for them, but detach yourself from them. The more detached you are from this world, the closer you will come to your spirit.

At your job, strive to be the best that you can be. However, there is a fine line between working responsibly and becoming a workaholic. So many hours are put into work that you become insecure when you finally get some time off. Without work, you do not know what to do. You immediately go back to work, just because it is familiar. This is not a good habit. It is an insecurity. You should detach yourself from work, in order to spend time with your soul.

We give high priority to our physical bodies these days. Genetic engineers are trying to find out how to expand the physical life of a human being. Scientists are creating super drugs for the longevity and vitality of the body. Instead of exercising for half an hour a day, super athletes exercise for several hours a day. The human body is the temple of God. We need to take care of it. However, we should not get overattached to it and forget about the soul. Learn to detach yourself from the body and spend time with the soul. The physical body, after all, is temporary; it comes from dust and returns to dust. Your soul is eternal.

Recently, gourmet foods have become readily available. The richer, tastier and more exotic the dish, the higher the price. It is very easy to get overattached to food. Food is a necessity for you and your family; enjoy it to the fullest. However, do not overdo it. Overeating and high cholesterol diets are extremely damaging to your body. When your body suffers, your soul suffers as well. If you die before the time span of the life that was given to you, you do a great injustice to your soul. Control the desire of your tongue. Eat to live a long and happy life. Don't live to eat and die before your time.

People today spend far too much time watching the television set. The television transmits all kinds of vibrations to the soul. Some can do harm. Watch TV occasionally; there is nothing wrong with enjoying your life. Nevertheless, do not become attached to it. Spend a quarter of the amount of your daily TV time on your soul. You will gain a lot from it. Remember, your soul is the only part of you that is eternal.

Advancements in the technological fields have produced intriguing toys for the intellect. Internet technology especially is taking up a large portion of our time. It is necessary to know how to work with this technology, but beware: it can become addictive. It is actually possible for the intellect to become completely possessed by computer technology.

The intellect searches out one opportunity after another, if not the computer, then books, classes, and so on. It is essential to get an education, but don't overdo it. Sometimes it is very difficult to steer your intellect in the right direction because of the intellectual ego. The intellect, like the lower brain, has many forms of ego gratification. Have the courage to maintain your balance. When you are expanding your intellectual knowledge, you must also learn to detach yourself from the intellect in order to devote time to your soul.

Learn to be detached while journeying on earth. This is a temporary place for us; it is but a short passage to eternity. If you follow the desires of your senses all the time, your soul will end up suffering. Take some time to contemplate the senses.

Train your eyes to be controlled by the soul. Do not allow your eyes to control your soul. Filter out all the bad habits of your eyes. Stop chasing everyone and everything. Your eyes must be steered by love, purity and spiritual search.

Our ears have incredible potential. They can help you achieve spiritual growth or they can cause a great deal of harm to the soul. If you let your soul control your ears, you will definitely grow. Tune your ears to hear the vibrations inside your heart. This internal process is very meditative. If your ears are tuned to the outer world, you will pick up the seeds of spiritual deterioration. Gossip, coarse language, hyperactive music, and loud noises will only hinder your growth. If you must listen to outside noise, be selective. Listen to classical music, poetry, soft tones, spiritual literature, and nature. Detach your ears completely from negative elements.

Always remember that your family is comprised of individual souls who are on a journey towards the spiritual world. You have no claim over them whatsoever. Provide for them in a detached manner. This will make it easy for your soul to approach the unknown.

One of the rewards of practicing detachment becomes apparent when we are about to die. Our transition from this world to the next will be easy if we have learned to let go. If we cannot let go of our wealth and family for a single day, how can we do so permanently? The lesson of detachment is one that nature wants us to learn through our free will. When the time comes for us to go, everything will be taken away from us. We can either go easily or attempt a futile resistance. So, as much as possible, become detached from the world.

Open your Eyes

Existence heaps thousands of opportunities in front of you to help your spiritual growth. It is important for you to be open to them. An important lesson may come in the form of a book, a friend or a loving animal.

A Sufi is one who is on the path of spiritual learning. Contemplate the following story of Hassan, a great Sufi mystic. When Hassan was very close to death, somebody asked him,

"Hassan, please tell us who your master was." He said, "I am dying. There is no time left for me. It is too late to ask me this question." The inquirer said, "You are still breathing, talking. Please tell me the name and I will not bother you." Hassan said, "I cannot give you one name because I had hundreds of masters. If I give you the name of all my masters, it will take months.

However, I will give you the names of three masters. One of my masters was a thief. Once I got lost in the desert, and, by the time I got to the village, it was very late. Half the night had passed and most of the townspeople had gone to sleep. The streets were completely empty; I was alone walking in a village, far from home. After a while I saw a man making a hole in the wall of a house. I asked him if there was a place where I could go to rest. He said, 'It seems that you are a Sufi mystic and, I think you should know that I am a thief.' He continued, 'It would be very difficult for you to find a place to stay at this hour, but you can stay with me if you are willing to stay with a thief.'

I considered the dilemma, but then it occurred to me that if the thief was not afraid of a Sufi, then I did not need to be afraid of the thief. So I said, 'Okay, I will join you.' I took shelter with the thief. This man was so compassionate that I lived with him for a month. Each night he would repeat to me, 'It is time for me to go to work. You take it easy, meditate, and do your work.' When the thief returned, I would ask him, 'Did you get anything today?' He sometimes said, 'Not today, but I shall try again tomorrow.' He was always in a state of hopefulness. For many weeks the thief would come home with nothing, but he was always joyful. He continued to tell me, 'I will try again.'

Hassan went on, "When I was meditating for long periods, sometimes for years, nothing happened. There were times when I was disappointed. I thought I should give up meditation; it didn't work. There is no such thing as God and all this meditation is a waste of time. Then I would remember the thief, who would repeat to me every night, 'With God's grace it will happen tomorrow.' So I tried one more time. If the thief had so much hope and optimism, the least I could do was try one more time. And the thief kept me going until one day it happened: I experienced the glory of God. At that moment, I bowed down in the direction of the thief's house. This optimistic thief was my first master."

Hassan continued, "My second master was a dog. One day I was feeling thirsty and was making my way towards a river. When I reached the river, I saw a dog that was also thirsty. Every time the dog looked into the river, he saw his own reflection and thought there was another dog. He barked and his reflection barked back. He would back away and then return to the river because he was afraid of his reflection. Eventually his thirst became so strong that he jumped into the water and the image disappeared. He drank the water, swam in the water, and became one with the water. I knew that through the dog a message had come to me from God. The message was that we have to jump into the unknown to overcome our fears. When I was poised to dive into the unknown, fear held me back. Then I remembered the dog; he had jumped in - why couldn't I? So one day I jumped into the river of the unknown. On that day all my fears vanished. That dog was my second master."

Hassan proceeded, "My third master was a small child. Once I saw a small child walking with a candle in his hands. He was taking the candle to a mosque. I asked the little child, 'Where is the flame that lit your candle?' The boy laughed and blew the candle out. Then he asked me, 'You just saw the light go out. Where has it gone?' At that moment, my preconceptions were shattered and my knowledge was shaken. Since then, I let go of all my false knowledge."

So Hassan talked about three masters. Then he said, "Existence gave me hundreds of masters but I have no more time left to tell you."

What does it mean to be a seeker? It means that one must be open to learning. You must make yourself available to existence. You will be put in a fortunate situation where a message will be illustrated. God is very compassionate. He continues to send us revelations through teachers disguised as friends, animals, and family members. But you will only see them if you open your inner eyes.

Get in tune with nature. Think of nature as your master. The more open you are to nature, the more you become aware of its beauty. Your level of intimacy will increase; your expression of love towards the unknown will increase. You will become more committed to the higher self. The more open you become to each individual element of nature, the deeper will be your understanding of the whole universe. Open yourself completely.

Be open to God. He wants to exist in your heart. But first you must learn from the simple lessons He wishes to teach you. Before we achieve a higher understanding of God, we must comprehend the simple lessons that God wishes to teach us.

If we cannot be completely open to esoteric learning, let's start by being a little open to God. We must start slowly, and gradually extend our comprehension. God teaches us one step at a time, provided we want to learn.

God is not in a hurry. He was always present and will always be present. God is eternity. His clock goes on ticking forever. We are the ones who are running out of time. Our spirits have traveled far; our souls are thirsty. It is time for us to mature. The time has come for us to open our books and learn the lessons of divinity. The only way this is possible is through an open mind and an open heart.

Judge Not

Jesus Christ says, "Judge Not." These two words have a very profound meaning behind it. As human beings, we find it almost impossible to refrain from making judgements. Judging has become second nature to us. We have a tendency to form opinions on issues that don't relate to us without even checking the facts.

Every time the mind pronounces a judgement call, the soul stops growing.

Judge not

A judgement is a lethal dose of poison that can do irreversible damage to your soul. It takes a great amount of courage to attempt to control the ego that judges constantly. The following test will make you aware of how many judgements you form without thinking. For one week, find half an hour every evening when you can reflect on the events that took place during the day. From the time you wake up, go through the whole day until the evening. Repeat each event to yourself in your mind. Do this exercise for one week and write down all the details. You may be surprised at your results at the end of the day.

Contemplate the following beautiful story. This story took place in China; the master Lao-Tzu loved to tell it. It has been repeated from generation to generation.

Once upon a time, in a small village in China, there lived an old man.

The man was very poor, but the kings envied him because he had a beautiful white horse. This horse was so captivating that the kings offered the old man vast sums to purchase it. But the old man would say, "This horse is very valuable to me. He is like a human, and how can you trade a human being for money? He is my friend, not something you can claim to own." The man faced great poverty; he was tempted, but he kept the horse.

One day he discovered that the horse was not in the stable. The people from the village said, "You crazy old man, we knew this was going to happen! We knew your horse would be stolen some day. You were offered immense wealth for the horse but you were stubborn. You were not able to protect the horse and now he is gone forever. This is a curse, a tragedy."

The old man replied, "Don't leap to conclusions. Simply observe the fact that the horse cannot be seen in the stable. That is the only visible fact; anything and everything else is a judgement."

The crowd replied, "We know what is going on. We are not claiming to be philosophers. The fact is that a priceless jewel has been lost and it is a great tragedy."

The old man replied, "The only fact that is clear to me is that the stable is empty. Beyond this I do not know anything else. Who knows what will happen next?"

People thought the old man had gone crazy. They started making fun of him. They always thought that he was not wise; if he had been, he would have sold the horse and lived comfortably. The old man decided that he would make a living as a woodcutter, bringing the wood from the forest and selling it. After several days, the horse returned.

He had run off into the wilderness. Amazingly, he brought several wild horses with him. Once again the people came together and said, "Old man, it seems that you were right and we were wrong. This incident turned out to be a blessing. Please accept our apologies."

The old man replied, "Once again, you are going too far. The only clear fact is that the horse has returned and has brought other horses back with him. Only God knows whether it is a blessing or not."

This time the crowd did not say much; they thought it possible that the old man was right. They kept silent but thought to themselves that, with a little training, the beautiful horses could all be sold for a great price.

The old man had only one child, a young boy. He was given the job of training the wild horses. After a few days, he fell off a horse and broke his legs. Once again the people gathered and naturally started judging the incident. They said, "Maybe you were right; the horse's return was a misfortune. You have only one son, and he has lost his legs. You are so old; he could have supported you. Now you are destitute."

The old man replied, "You still continue to judge too quickly. The only thing that is clear is that my son has broken his legs. Who knows whether it is a blessing or a curse?"

Soon after, the country was involved in a war with its neighbour. All the young men were forced to join the military. The only young man left behind was the old man's crippled son. The people gathered and wept because from every house all the sons were forced into battle. There was no possibility of their coming back - the opposing army was too strong.

The crowd came to the old man and wept for their young ones. They said to the old man, "You were absolutely right. This is a blessing for you. Maybe your son is crippled, but he is still with you. Our sons are gone forever. Your son will eventually start to walk again; you are so lucky."

The old man replied, "It is very frustrating to talk to you people. Once again you are judging. The only fact that is clear is that your sons are forced into battle and my son is not. But who knows whether it is a blessing or a misfortune. Only God knows why this is happening."

Our way of thinking is very similar to that of the crowd. When we go to work, we judge. When we are dealing with family situations, we judge. When we socialize, we judge. Remember that you cannot judge a book by its cover. You cannot judge a sentence from a single word. Life comes in fragments.

We receive one piece at a time. Judgement can only be applied to the total. Only God knows the total.

Service to Mankind

When God is pleased with us, He gives us a golden opportunity to grow spiritually. This opportunity is service. Throughout history, many individuals have provided service to mankind. The more service you provide, the closer you will come to your Creator. Whenever you provide service to others, do it voluntarily. True service means to help without receiving anything in return.

When we look at the history of humankind, we see that there have always been opportunities for service. Soldiers have died for the independence of their country. Doctors have dedicated themselves to those suffering. Research scientists devote their energy to the discovery of a cure for a deadly disease. Messengers of God put their life in jeopardy to preach the laws of God. A nun sacrifices her life to assist those in need.

You do not need to have professional qualifications to serve. There is always something you can offer to society. When you are at work, see if you can help others for an extra hour, or maybe you can offer them a ride home. If there are no opportunities at work, give your service to a hospital as a volunteer for a few hours a week. Senior's homes also appreciate an extra hand. Try doing some community work; it will be spiritually rewarding.

When we look at the immense sacrifices that prophets and sages made to teach us the principles of God, we realize how voluntary their task was. None of the prophets claimed any wealth in return for the service they provided. They did not say, "Until I get paid I will not deliver divine guidance." They served God unconditionally.

When you serve God, you must do so unconditionally. Do not serve with the intention of receiving something in return. Certainly, if you serve, you will be rewarded. Your actions will definitely bear fruit. However do not engage in service as a tactic to achieve another end. That is not real service.

Many people choose a career that will enable them to serve their country. They sacrifice their lives, family, and wealth in order to serve. A policeman working in the homicide division shows great courage. It is a difficult and demanding job. Why does an individual want to become a homicide detective? Why choose to endure all kinds of physical, mental, and emotional abuse. One of the main reasons is to provide service to society. It is easy to walk away, but someone has to do it. The brave spirit is willing to serve unconditionally.

Similarly, psychologists, doctors, nurses, policemen, and others who deal with life and death situations have the courage to serve society. Individuals who serve in such sensitive areas deserve respect. Often, they require hours of psychotherapy to face the demands of their job. Their spirits are great warriors.

Each individual goes to work for a number of reasons. Obviously, the main reason is to provide for yourself and your family. You put in the required hours and leave at the end of the day. However, if you go beyond the requirements of your job description, this will set you apart from the others. For example, if we compare two psychotherapists, there would doubtlessly be some similarities. They both provide professional guidance. They both charge money for their services. They are both effective. However, one has decided to devote an extra hour at no cost. This extra step immediately benefits the spiritual state of the therapist. Both therapists are earning a living honestly, but only one has made spiritual strides by offering voluntary service. So give a few extra hours of service to humankind. By serving your community, you are serving God. God has no shape, form, or colour. How will you find Him, if you want to serve Him? The way to serve God is by serving God's creatures.

If the prophets did not serve God by preaching to humankind, society would be non-existent. There would be no code of ethics, no law and order. If there were no doctors, we would not survive. If no one chooses to become a policeman, who would protect us? In every context, there are individuals who go beyond their required duty to provide service. When you provide unconditional service, you illuminate an inner light. It is difficult to convey the joy you experience.

We all benefit from the services that have been provided by others. We benefit from the wisdom of the prophets and sages. We enjoy the independence of our country, ensured by brave soldiers. We do not have to worry unduly about crime; we have a responsible police force. We do not have to save lives since doctors are available. We do not have to worry about all the things that others are providing for us. It is time for us to return the service that we have taken for granted. From today onwards, we will find a way to serve God by serving His creatures on earth.

Life is a Paradox

Existence has created opposite extremes for us to experience: man and woman, life and death, summer and winter, night and day, hot and cold, failure and progress, positive and negative, good and bad, suffering and pleasure, yin and yang, happiness and sadness, doubt and certainty and so on. From a spiritual point of view, we should consider these opposites as constructive complements and not as destructive oppositions. They are two sides of the same coin.

When a man and a woman get married, they will experience the contrasts of extremes. They will have times of sadness and happiness, failure and progress, wealth and poverty, suffering and pleasure. The husband is at one end of a spectrum, he is purely masculine. The wife is at the other end of the spectrum, she is completely feminine. The husband needs the gentle, feminine side of his wife to reach the centre. The wife needs the sterner qualities of her husband to encourage her to come to the centre.

We are born with both a mother and a father, male and female, passive and aggressive; we are a product of both masculine and feminine genes. The reason a man needs his wife is because her gentleness and compassion will enter the man's heart. They will nourish the seeds of gentleness that are hidden deep inside the heart of a man. Likewise, the characteristics of a husband will enter the heart of his wife. They will enable her to achieve more spiritual harmony. The physical woman helps the man find his inner gentle side. The physical man helps the woman balance her femininity and move closer to spirituality.

Before you experience spiritual light, you must experience darkness. Otherwise, how will you know the difference? You must experience the chill of winter before you can appreciate the warmth of summer. If you are not given the chance to experience the darkness of the night, how will you be able to compare it to the brightness of day? If you have tasted sadness, you will love the flavour of happiness.

All aspects of life have opposite extremes. During your lifetime, you will experience both. In you personal life, you will face many disappointments with your loved ones. You will also cherish unforgettable moments of joy. While you are in the process of educating yourself, there will be times of disappointment and success. Your health will be good at times, and bad at other times. Money will come and money will go. When a person goes from adverse conditions to better ones, the latter will be cherished profoundly. A man who goes from rags to riches will be in a position to appreciate his wealth. A person who is born rich and remains rich will not appreciate it as much.

Before we can experience spiritual bliss, we must experience spiritual desolation. We must experience sadness, darkness, unhappiness, unconsciousness, and unenlightenment. After we have endured these negative extremes, we are ready to experience the other extreme. After sadness, comes spiritual happiness. Unconsciousness becomes consciousness; unenlightenment surrenders to enlightenment.

If we all began life as enlightened entities, how would we compare spiritual light to darkness? It would not be possible. We would take enlightenment for granted. This is why we must go from unenlightenment to enlightenment, from darkness to eternal light.

The seed of enlightenment is in our hearts. Our experience of unenlightenment, darkness, and unconsciousness will force the seed of enlightenment to grow. The dark side of the soul will disappear into the bright light of spiritual bliss. When all dualities disappear, enlightenment is the result.

In order for us to blossom spiritually, we must learn to accept both extremes of our lives: positive and negative, good and bad, right and wrong. If we only accept one aspect willingly, we will be forced to learn to accept the other. Be open and accepting to both extremes. At some point during our journey of the soul, all dualities will merge into the seed of enlightenment. One who reaches to this stage will be part of the universal consciousness.